Gacha for beginners

By Jessica Bendle

Amazon Kindle Edition

About the author

Jessica Bendle is an artist and an author.

She has a YouTube channel called

KittyWitty123.

To contact her please email.

cbendle57@gmail.com.

Contents:

<u>Chapter 1</u>

Downloading the apps:

Make sure that, before you start,
you have a smartphone or tablet that can take screenshots.
Now go to the app store on your phone
or tablet and download the following apps:
Gacha life;
Kinemaster;
Cute Cut;
Ibis Paint X;
IV recorder;
YT Studio;
Now that you have downloaded all of the apps
above, you can start making gacha videos.

Chapter 2

How to make a video.

It's time to make a video! So, let's learn how to make one.

Go to gacha life;

Press "Studio";

Tap one of the characters at the bottom;

Change their size by pressing

either the plus or minus buttons;

Tap the screen to move your character;

Tap "pose" to put your character into

the position you want; Press the X;

Press "BG" to choose a background;

Press "Props" to choose some props for the

background to make it more interesting;

Press "Hide";

Take a screenshot;

Keep on doing this over and over,

until you have enough screenshots for a video!

You can also make people talk,

have multiple characters

in a scene, and loads more!

Once you have your screenshots,

go to kinemaster to make your video.

Please send me your email address
and
I will send you the free link on
how to do this and how to make a great

Oc.

Chapter 3

How to make a thumbnail/edit a gacha Oc

Making a thumbnail may sound hard,

but it's actually really easy!

There are also quite a few benefits that you

gain from putting one on your video too.

It looks professional,

your video gets more views, and their super fun to
make.

The app I make thumbnails on is on a free app

called Ibis Paint X.

Here's what I do:

Go to Gacha Life;

Choose the character(s) that

you want in the thumbnail;

Go to "Studio" and take a screenshot of them

in the outfits and positions you want

(the background must be yellow);

Now go to Ibis Paint X;

Select "My Gallery";

Tap the plus symbol in the bottom left;

Tap either "16:9" or "9:16";

Select the "1" in the bottom left;

Press the camera;

Select the screenshot you took earlier;

Move it to where you want on the canvas

then tap the green tick

(your image doesn't have to fill the whole screen);

When you get the notification

"Extract Line Drawing"

select "Cancel";

Select the top "layer"

(It's the pink and white one);

Tap the screen;

Use a pinching motion with your thumbs

to zoom in and out;

Tap the brush icon on the bottom left;

Select "Magic brush";

Tap on every part of the hair
so it's all blue then tap the
"S";

Touch and hold the first layer then bring

it above your screenshot layer;

Tap the screen;

Select the button in the very left bottom corner;

Tap and hold the hair;

Select the bottom middle button;

Move the slider down so it's a darker colour;

Select the bottom middle again;

Now you can start shading the hair;

All I do for backgrounds is:

Create a new layer by pressing the plus;

Tap and hold the layer

so it's at the

very bottom;

Tap the screen,

then the bottom middle button;

Select the colour that you

want for your background;

Select the bottom middle button again;

Tap the pen;

Tap the 2nd pen;

Select the felt tip pen;

Move the blue slider

all the way up;

Tap the screen;

Colour in the whole background;

Tap the 1st and 2nd pen again;

Select any soft pen;

Tap the screen;

Select a colour that isn't close to

your background colour;

Tap the screen;

Now put dots of colour

all aroundthe screen

(Canvas); Tap the 3 squares

at the bottom

(there's usually a number on the first square);

Select the 3 dots;

Choose the option

"Save canvas as transparent PNG";

Now you're done!

Chapter 4

How to make an intro and outro

Your intro and your outro

are possibly one of the

most important things

on your channel,

as they will be shown

at the start and end of every video.

But there's no need to fear,

as making them is fun and easy!

Open gacha life;

Select one of your characters;

Tap "Body";

Now tap "Change";

Select "Animated";

Choose an animated pose;

Tap "X";

Tap "X" again;

Choose the green background;

Now open V recorder;

Go back to gacha life;

Press the "Zoom" button;

Now press the "Hide" button;

Select the orange circle

and press the red circle;

Choose the 2nd highest quality

of recording;

Select "Start Now";

Keep recording until your

happy with the video length;

Now press the orange circle again;

Press the red square;

Search for a copy-right free background

that fits your recording and screenshot it;

Open kinemaster;

Create a new video by

pressing the big red button;

Select "16:9";

Go to media;

"Screenshots";

Choose the background

you screenshotted

earlier; Press the tick

in the right-hand corner;

Tap the picture, then "Crop";

Zoom into it on "Start Position";

Now press "End Position" and zoom

into a different area on the

other side of the screen;

Press the tick in the right hand corner again;

Press "Layer" then "Media";

Choose the video you took before;

Tap the tick mark in the top right;

Press and hold the video and move it to the start;

Cut it so it's about the same length as the background;

Tap the video again and select "Cropping";

Crop out the orange circle and "V Recorder" logo;

Press the left facing arrow;

Go to "Chroma Key";

Tap "Enable";

Press the left facing arrow a 2nd time;

Tap the key button on the middle left;

Move the playhead (the red line) to the very left;

Place your character where
you want them to start;
Put the playhead a bit
before the end of your video;
Now move your character
where you want them to stop;
Tap the tick on the top right corner;
Tap the whitish square;
Choose any transition;
Select how long the transition lasts;
Press the tick mark;
Rinse and repeat;
When you're finished, add music
(you cannot monetize your YouTube
videos with this music) and export it!

For the outro:

Open gacha life;
Choose your main Oc and then click
"Background"; Choose the neon green background:

Now press "Body" and select the hashtag (#) in the top
left;

Press "Body sheet 1" and take a screenshot

(If your Oc has a tail or is holding something,

also take a screenshot of "Body sheet 2");

Go to Ibis Paint X;

Separate all of the body parts into different layers,

then press "Save layer as transparent PNG" on all of them;

Now go to "Cute Cut";

Press the plus (+) symbol in the top left;

Tap "Create";

Select the same neon green I showed

you earlier as the background colour;

Choose "Done";

Tap another plus (+) symbol;

Select "Photo" and click the hair screenshot;

Tap the plus underneath and again press

"Photo"; Now select the body screenshot;

Keep on doing this until you

have the whole Oc done;

Double tap the hair screenshot

and position it;

Do this with the rest of the body

parts until the Oc looks good;

Double tap the hair screenshot
again and press the blue wand:

Select the plus (+) and then "Custom transition";

Tap the 2nd arrow and then move the blue

circle in the middle so it's on your Oc's forehead;

Now tap and hold onto the bottom left corner

of the screen and move your hair to the left;

Select the plus (+) and custom transition again;

Choose the 1st arrow this time;

Now tap and hold the bottom right and move the hair right;

Continue to move the body parts until your satisfied;

Export the video (see page 14);

Take a screenshot of a background;

Go to kinemaster;

Make a new video;

Click "Media then "Screenshots";

Choose the background you took;

Tap the tick in the top right;

Tap "Layer" then "Media";

Press "Export" then select your video;

Now press "Chroma Key" and "Enable";

Now select the arrow in the top right-hand corner;

Move your Oc to the left

(we do this so you can have links at the end of your video);

Now add music and export the video.

To add them to your video.

Once you have finished your video,

and before you export it, go to the start and

press "Media" and then "Export";

Click your intro;

Do the same thing for the outro but

go the end of your video instead of the start;

Yay! You've made an intro and an outro!

Give yourself a pat on the back, you deserve it.

Now we can move on to...

Chapter 5

How to post a video to YouTube and add a thumbnail

This is by far the most important step,
because it is how people will find
and/or watch your gacha videos!

Go to your YouTube account and change it

to the channel you want to upload your video on

(you don't need to do this step if you only have one

YouTube account on your phone/tablet);

Open up your file's app;

Click "Videos" and select the video you want to
upload;

Press "Share" and select "Share to YouTube";

Enter your title, the description,
and anything else you want to add;

To add the thumbnail:

While your video is uploading to YouTube, open YT
Studio;

Tap on the video;

Click the pencil button;

Tap "Edit thumbnail" then "Custom thumbnail";
Find the thumbnail you made and

tap it; Press "Select" and done.

Chapter 6

How to export videos

In cute cut:

Once you have made your video,

it's time to export it Tap the button that

looks like a square with an arrow inside of it;

Select the quality you want.

In kinemaster:

Click the button that looks like a line

with 3 dots on it; Choose the video quality.

Congratulations! You've finished the book!

If you have read all of this book, you, reader, are ready to...

Make gacha videos;

Make an intro and outro;

Edit videos;

Edit characters;

Use complicated apps like cute cut;

Create amazing Oc's;

Delve into the gacha and YouTube community;

And most importantly, have fun doing all these things!

You have now successfully learned more
about gacha then most people do when starting off!

I hope you had as much fun reading this as I did
making it.

<u>Please read</u>

Due to copyright reasons,

there are no pictures of

gacha characters in this book...

My YouTube channel is called

KittyWitty123, and

it is completely free,

if you would like to watch any of my videos!

Printed in Great Britain
by Amazon